My Life as an Immigrant

Nancy Kelly Allen

rourkeeducationalmedia.com

Scan for Related Titles and Teacher Resources

www.rourkeeducationalmedia.com

PHOTO CREDITS: Cover: © subjug, Bill Noll, franckreporter; All interior images courtesy of the Library of Congress.

Edited by: Precious McKenzie
Cover design by: Tara Raymo
Interior design by: Renee Brady

Library of Congress PCN Data

My Life as an Immigrant / Nancy Kelly Allen
(Little World Social Studies)
ISBN 978-1-61810-142-6 (hard cover)(alk. paper)
ISBN 978-1-61810-275-1 (soft cover)
Library of Congress Control Number: 2011945869

Also Available as:

Rourke Educational Media
Printed in the United States of America,
North Mankato, Minnesota

rourkeeducationalmedia.com
customerservice@rourkeeducationalmedia.com • PO Box 643328 Vero Beach, Florida 32964

I am an **immigrant**. Immigrants are people who leave their **native** land to live in another **country**.

In 1900, my family sailed from **Italy** to **America** across the wild and stormy Atlantic Ocean.

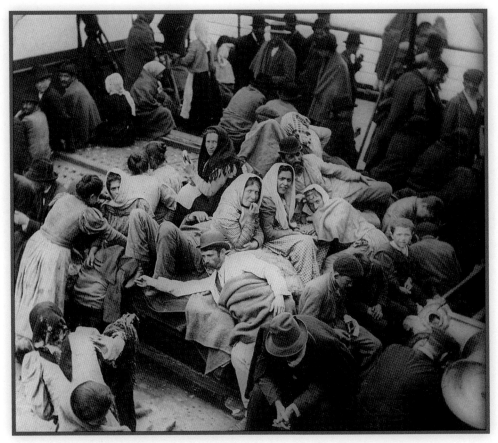

Immigrants were crowded onto boats going to America.

The Statue of Liberty welcomed immigrants to America.

Our first stop was Ellis Island in New York. Two doctors checked our health.

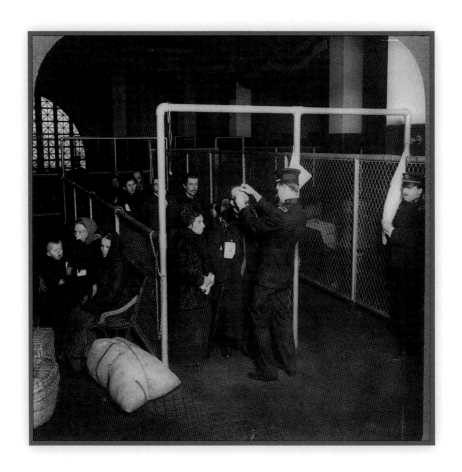

Ellis Island was the entry station for immigrants coming to America.

Mama and Papa had to take reading tests. They passed. What a relief!

If immigrants failed the tests, they could not enter the United States of America.

Like most immigrants, we came to America for freedom and opportunities. We wanted to make a better life.

Some immigrant women earned a living by typing.

Many immigrants stayed in large cities because they could find jobs there. Papa found a job in a meat market in New York City.

New York grew into a bustling city as more immigrants moved to America.

My older brother got a job on the railroad. He moved to one of the new towns that grew along the railroad tracks in the American **West**.

Some immigrants traveled westward across the country on trains.

At school, I learned to speak English with students from 25 different countries.

From 1880 to 1923, about 23 million immigrants came to America to live and work.

We also did work at home for extra money. For fun, I played games in the street.

Tag and jacks were favorite street games.

Coming to America has been exciting.
There is so much to see and do.

The United States of America is called a melting pot because immigrants came here from so many different countries.

Picture Glossary

 **America** (uh-MER-i-kuh): Another name for the United States of America.

 **country** (KUHN-tree): A part of the world with its own borders.

 **immigrant** (IM-uh-gruhnt): A person who leaves a native land to live in another country.

Italy (IT-uh-lee): A country in Europe from which many immigrants came.

native (NAY-tuv): Belonging to a particular place by birth.

West (WEST): Land in the western part of the United States that was the last to be settled.

Index

Websites

www.ellisisland.org/immexp/wseix_4_3.asp?

www.teacher.scholastic.com/activities/immigration/tour/stop1.htm

www.pbskids.org/bigapplehistory/immigration/topic7.html

About the Author

Nancy Kelly Allen has lived in Kentucky all her life. Her great-great-great grandparents were immigrants who sailed from Ireland to America. They landed on the Virginia coast and traveled to Kentucky. Nancy was born about 150 years later.

Meet The Author!
www.meetREMauthors.com